Make It with Felt

by
DONNA LAWSON

Inside illustrations by the author

Cover illustration by Margo Hrubec

SCHOLASTIC BOOK SERVICES
New York Toronto London Auckland Sydney Tokyo

Contents

ISBN 0-590-31804-7

12 11 10 9 8 7 6 5 4 3 2 1   2 3 4 5 6/8

Making Gifts with Felt

Felt! You'll love this material because it's so easy to work with. You can glue it or sew it. In minutes you can make a gift. And it won't cost you much money either.

You can make all the gifts in this book out of the 9-by-12-inch pieces of felt you can buy in your local dime store. They come in a rainbow of colors, and you can use them to make these great gifts for holidays and birthdays.

Follow the directions for making each gift. But use some of your own ideas too. If you want to, change the colors of the felt or the decorations on a gift. Working with felt is quick and easy, and this book should give you lots of ideas for making your own designs.

Once you decide on a gift to make, be sure to collect all the equipment and material you'll need before you start to work. And *don't miss* the tips and how-to's on pages 4 and 5. They'll help you to make better gifts and have more fun doing it.

Tips on...

Gluing Felt

Use only white glue (Sobo or Elmer's). If you use felt made with polyester (polyfelt), use only a little glue so it doesn't come through the felt. Use a piece of scrap to test how much glue you'll need on the polyfelt. Felt made of a wool mix is easier to use on gifts that need gluing.

Tracing and Cutting Patterns

Use a piece of tracing paper a little bigger than the pattern you are going to trace. Hold the paper down over the pattern and trace over all the lines with a pencil. Pin the tracing paper onto the felt. Cut out the pattern along the pencil lines. Remove the pins.

Sewing

Sew with a single thread, unless the directions tell you to use a double thread.

Knot the end of the thread, unless the directions tell you not to.

How to...

Sew on a Button

Use chalk to mark the place where the button is to be sewn. Make a knot on the end of the thread. Push the needle through the felt from the front and pull the thread through. Bring the needle back up through the felt and into one of the holes in the button. Push the needle down through the other hole and into the felt. Pull the thread through. Keep doing this until the button is secure.

Fasten the thread by taking several small stitches in place on the back. Then cut the thread.

Make a Running Stitch

Make a knot on the end of the thread. Push the needle through the felt from the back. Pull the thread through. Weave the needle in and out of the felt. Keep the stitches all the same size — about ⅛ inch — if you can.

Fasten the thread, at the end of the sewing, by making two small stitches in the same place. Then push the needle through to the back and cut off the thread.

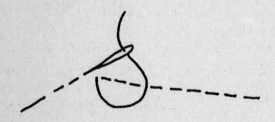

Make an Overcast Stitch

Make a knot on the end of the thread. Push the needle through the felt from the front. Pull the thread through. Bring the needle back over the edge. Insert the needle in the same place the thread went through the first time. Pull the thread through. Bring the needle over the edge again. This time insert the needle ¼ inch to the side of the first stitch. Keep repeating this last step.

Fasten the thread, at the end of the sewing, by making two overcast stitches in the same place. Push the needle through to the back and cut off the thread.

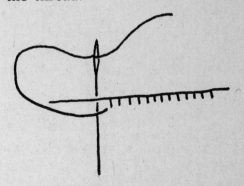

Flower Pin

You can turn this flower pin into a pretty hair ornament by sewing on the bobby pin. Or you can make it a piece of bright costume jewelry by sewing on the safety pin.

It's so easy, you can make lots of these flower pins — in lots of different colors.

You'll need

a piece of orange felt 2½ by 2½ inches
a large, bright blue button (about 1 inch across) with sewing thread to match
a bobby pin *or* a safety pin
needle
pins
scissors
tracing paper and pencil

1. Make a pattern for the flower by tracing picture 1.

2. Pin the tracing to the felt.

3. Cut out the tracing and remove the pins.

4. Sew the button in the center of the flower (see page 4).

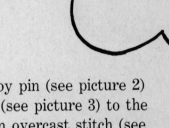

picture 1

5. Sew the straight side of the bobby pin (see picture 2) or the clip side of the safety pin (see picture 3) to the center back of the flower. Use an overcast stitch (see page 5).

picture 2

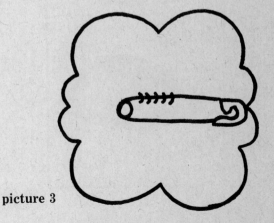

picture 3

Eyeglass Case Cover

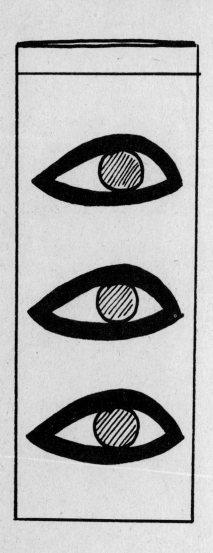

Here's a great gift for anyone you know who wears sunglasses or reading glasses.

You'll need

a piece of dark green felt 7 by 7 inches
a piece of black felt 4 by 6 inches
a piece of white felt 4 by 6 inches
scraps of purple, turquoise, pink, and light green felt
white glue
scissors
toothpick
pins
ruler
tracing paper and pencil

1. Spread glue evenly, with the toothpick, around three sides of the dark green felt. Keep the glue close to the edges (picture 1).

2. Fold the felt in half and press the glued edges together.

picture 1

3. Cut a piece of light green felt ½ inch by 3½ inches.

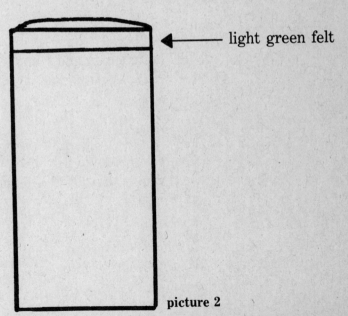

light green felt

4. Spread glue evenly on the back of the light green felt. Press it down firmly along the open edge on one side of the dark green felt (picture 2).

picture 2

9

5. Make 3 tracings of picture 3.

6. Pin the tracings to the black felt.

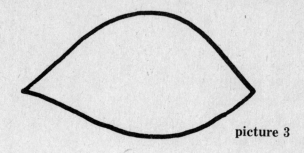

picture 3

7. Make 3 tracings of picture 4. Pin the tracings to the white felt.

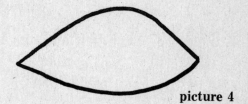

picture 4

8. Cut out all the tracings and remove the pins.

9. Measure down a ½ inch from the light green felt. Push a pin through the felt at this point.

10. Spread glue evenly on the back of one of the black eye shapes. Place it right below the pin (see picture 5).

11. Measure down ½ inch from the bottom of the first black eye shape and mark with a pin. Glue and press down the second black eye shape (see picture 5). Do the same with the third black eye shape.

12. Spread glue evenly on the back of one of the white eye shapes. Center it on the first black eye shape and press down. Do the same with the other two white eye shapes.

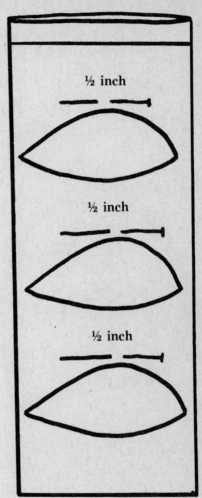

picture 5

13. For the eyeballs, use a nickel to make circles on the tracing paper. Pin the tracings to the scraps of felt and cut out. Make one pink eyeball, one purple eyeball, and one turquoise eyeball. Glue them down in the center of the white eye shapes.

11

Halloween Mask

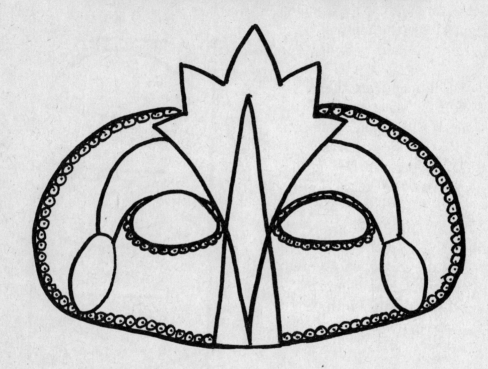

You'll need
a black eye mask (you can buy this in a dime store)
¾ yard of black sequins-on-a-strip
scraps of purple, lime-green, red, and yellow felt
scissors
pins
white glue
ruler
tracing paper and pencil

1. Cut a piece of sequins, 18 inches long, off the strip.

2. Carefully spread glue on the back of the 18-inch strip.

3. Starting at the bottom edge of the mask—on the bump of the nose—press the strip down around the edge of the mask (picture 1). Keep going until you come back to where you started. Cut off any extra sequins.

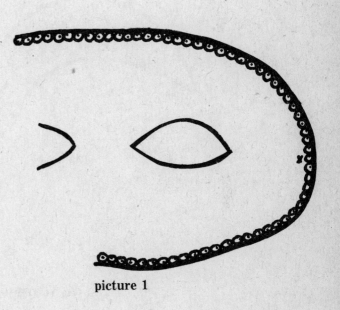

picture 1

4. Cut the leftover piece of sequins in half. Use these two pieces for the eyes. Spread glue on the back of one strip. Press it down around the edge of one eye. Do the same with the other piece of sequins.

5. For the decorations on the mask, trace the patterns on these two pages. Make two tracings of the eyebrow, the tear, and the nose side. Make only *one* tracing of the leaf and the nose strip.

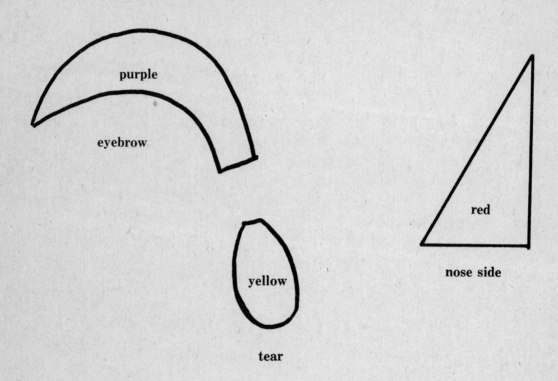

purple

eyebrow

yellow

tear

red

nose side

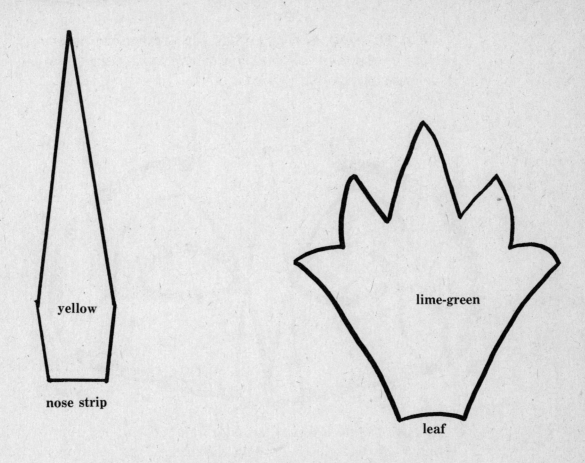

yellow

nose strip

lime-green

leaf

6. Pin the patterns to the felt. (See each pattern piece for color.) Cut out the patterns and remove the pins.

7. BEFORE YOU START TO GLUE: Arrange the decorations on the mask so you know where each piece belongs (picture 2).

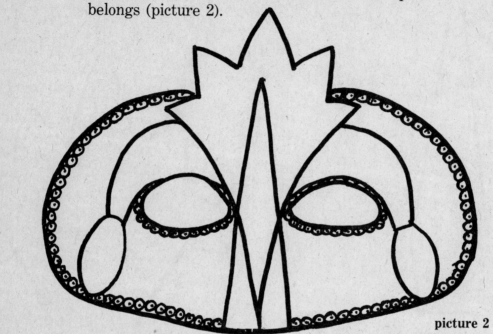

picture 2

8. Remove the decorations and start gluing with the eyebrows. Spread glue evenly on the back of the eyebrows and press them in place.

9. Glue a tear on the end of each eyebrow.

10. Spread glue on the leaf, but leave the top three points unglued. Press the leaf between the eyebrows so the three points are sticking up above the mask (picture 3).

picture 3

11. Glue the nose strip down the center of the nose. It should cover part of the leaf, and the bottom edge of the strip should be glued on top of the sequins.

12. The nose sides should be glued on either side of the nose strip. The tips should meet at the bottom (see picture 4).

picture 4

17

Notepad Cover

This is a useful gift to give any
time of the year.

You'll need

a piece of yellow felt 5 by 12 inches
a piece of brown felt 5 by 7 inches
scraps of turquoise, purple, yellow,
    and hot-pink felt
a notepad 4 by 6 inches (you can buy
    this in a dime or stationery store)
yellow thread
needle
scissors
white glue
ruler
tracing paper and pencil

1. Fold the yellow felt in half
   across the width.

2. With yellow thread, sew the
   sides together to make a pocket
   (picture 1). Use a small overcast
   stitch (see page 5).

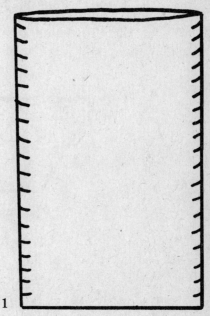

picture 1

3. Measure down ³/₄ inch from the open end of the pocket.
   Draw a line across the felt.

4. Measure down ³/₄ inch from one edge of the brown felt.
   Draw a line across the felt.

5. Spread glue evenly in the ³/₄-inch space on the brown felt. Glue the brown felt to the yellow felt within the ³/₄-inch space (see picture 2).

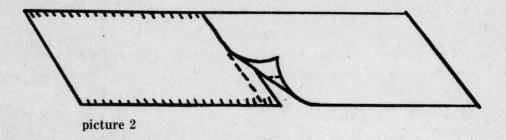

picture 2

6. Trace the flower patterns below.

hot-pink

turquoise

yellow

purple

yellow

7. Pin the tracings to the felt. (See each pattern piece for color.)

8. Cut out the tracings and remove the pins.

9. BEFORE YOU START TO GLUE: Arrange all the flower pieces on the notepad cover (picture 3).

picture 3

10. One at a time, remove each piece and spread glue on the back. Then press the piece back in place.

Picture Frame

This picture frame is just the thing to give—or get—on Valentine's Day.

You'll need

a piece of hot-pink felt 6 by 6 inches
a piece of cardboard 6 by 6 inches
a scrap of red felt
½ yard red rayon cord
6 sequins
small photograph (yours or a
    friend's) about 2½ by 3 inches

white glue
Scotch tape
scissors
pins
tracing paper and pencil

1. Trace the half-heart shape (picture 1).

2. Fold the pink felt in half. Pin the tracing to the felt. Place the dotted line on the fold.

3. Cut around the inside line first. (Cut across, but *not along*, the dotted line.)

4. Cut around the outside line. Remove the pins and open up the heart.

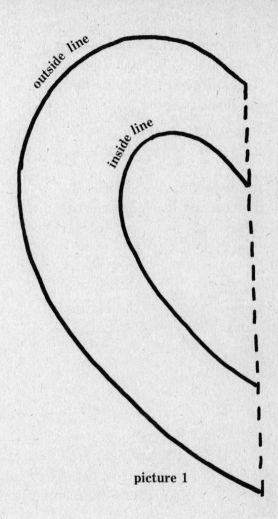

picture 1

5. Spread glue only on the point of the heart. Center the heart on the cardboard and press down on the point (picture 2).

6. Hold the felt down with your fingers and trace around the outside of the heart.

7. Carefully cut out the cardboard heart.

glue

picture 2

8. Spread glue evenly on the back of the photograph. Lift the felt heart and center the photograph in the opening. Press the photograph in place.

9. Lift the felt heart again. Spread glue evenly on the back. Press the heart in place.

10. Cut out 6 tiny hearts from the red felt. If you need a pattern for these, trace picture 3.

picture 3

11. Arrange the hearts all around the frame. Then glue them in place. Glue the sequins between the hearts.

12. Cut off 12 inches of red cord to go around the frame. The short piece left over will be used to hang the frame.

13. Spread glue carefully around the edge of the frame. Press the cord down on the glue. Start in the middle—at the top of the frame (picture 4). Cut off any extra cord.

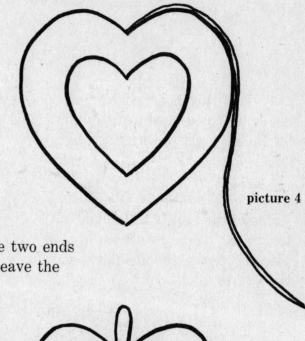

picture 4

14. Fold the short piece of cord in half. Tape the two ends down on the back of the frame (picture 5). Leave the loop sticking above the top of the frame.

picture 5

back

front

The Big Bookmark

Your favorite bookworm will love
to curl up with one of these.

You'll need

2 pieces of light-colored felt 11½ by 2½ inches
a piece of dark-colored felt 11 by 2 inches
scissors
white glue
ruler
tracing paper and pencil

1. Trace the letters and the exclamation point below. Use a separate piece of paper for each tracing.

2. Pin the tracings on one of the 11½-by-2½-inch pieces of light-colored felt.

3. Cut out the tracings.

   To cut out the openings in the B's and O's, fold
   the felt over. Make a small cut with the scissors
   where the opening is marked on the tracing. Unfold,
   and put the point of the scissors through the cut.
   Now you can cut around the inside line.

4. BEFORE YOU START TO GLUE: Arrange all the letters and the exclamation point on the dark piece of felt.

5. One at a time, spread glue on
   the back of each piece and press
   it in place.

6. Finally, glue the dark felt to the
   large piece of light felt. Make
   sure the border is even all the
   way around (picture 1).

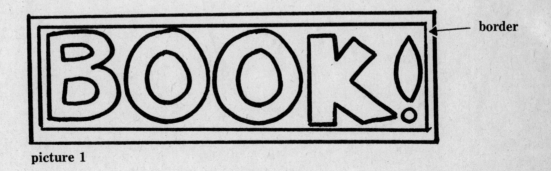

border

picture 1

Apple Shoulder Bag

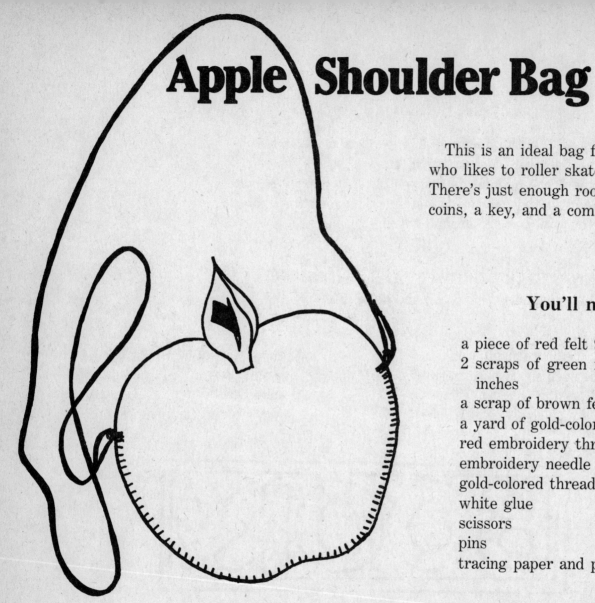

This is an ideal bag for anyone who likes to roller skate or jog. There's just enough room in it for coins, a key, and a comb.

You'll need

a piece of red felt 9 by 12 inches
2 scraps of green felt, each 2 by 2 inches
a scrap of brown felt 2 by 2 inches
a yard of gold-colored cord
red embroidery thread
embroidery needle
gold-colored thread
white glue
scissors
pins
tracing paper and pencil

1. Make two tracings of the half-
   apple pattern (picture 1).

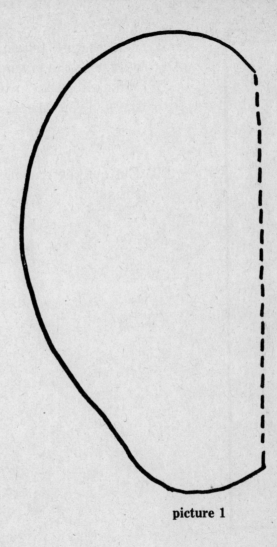

picture 1

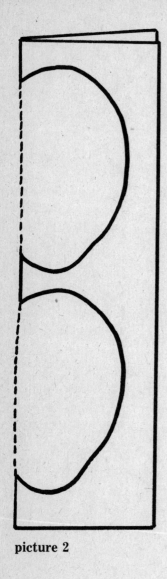

picture 2

2. Fold the red felt in half lengthwise. Pin the tracings to the felt. Make sure the dotted line is on the fold (picture 2).

3. Cut out the tracings and remove the pins.

4. Make two tracings of the leaf pattern (picture 3).

picture 3

5. Pin the tracings to the green felt. Cut out the tracings and remove the pins.

6. Make two tracings of the stem pattern (picture 4).

7. Pin the tracings to the brown felt and cut out. Remove the pins.

picture 4

8. Glue the two stem shapes together.

9. Glue the two leaf shapes together.

10. Glue the stem to the center top of one apple shape. And glue the leaf to the center top of the other apple shape.

11. Pin the apple shapes together with the stem and the leaf on the outside.

12. Use an overcast stitch (see page 5) to sew the bag together. With red embroidery thread, make the first stitch and pull it tight. Make the second stitch, but leave it loose. Slip one end of the gold cord through the loose stitch. Knot the cord around the thread, then pull the stitch tight (picture 5).

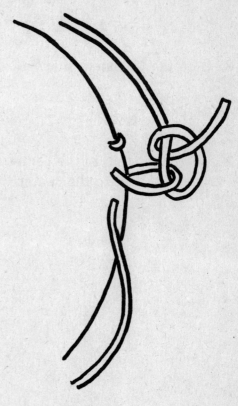

picture 5

13. Continue sewing around the apple shape until you have only two stitches to go. Make the first stitch loose. Slip the loose end of the gold cord through the stitch. Knot the cord, then pull the stitch tight. Make the last stitch and knot off the thread.

14. Use the gold-colored thread to wrap the short end of the gold cord neatly to the shoulder strap.

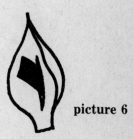

picture 6

15. Finally, fold the leaf over and make a small cut in the center of the leaf. Slip the stem through the leaf to hold the bag closed (picture 6).

Cat Beanbag

The purrfect gift for cat fans!

You'll need

2 pieces of black felt 7 by 9 inches

a piece of red felt 4 by 4 inches

2 small flat blue buttons

1 small flat red button

black, blue, and red sewing thread

1 pound of white beans — uncooked

white glue

needle

pins

scissors

tracing paper and pencil

white chalk

1. Trace the pattern for the cat's body (picture 1). Trace the solid and the dotted lines in the picture.

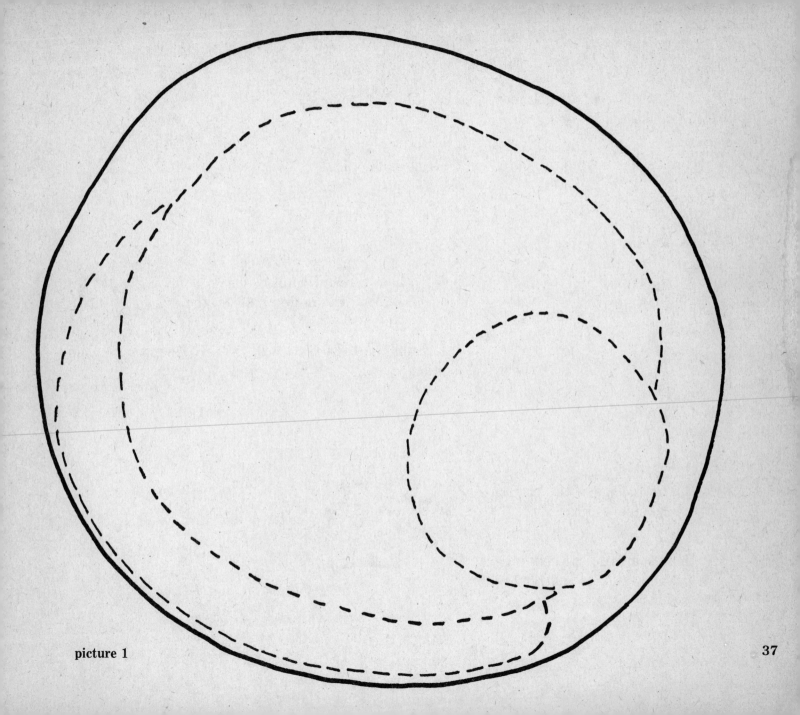

2. Put the two pieces of black felt together. Pin the tracing to the double thickness of felt.

3. Cut around the solid outside line *only*. Remove the pins.

4. Pin the tracing back on only *one* of the pieces of black felt.

5. With blue thread, doubled, make a running stitch (see page 5) along the dotted lines on the tracing.

6. Carefully pull off the tracing paper. Don't pull out any stitches.

7. Make two tracings of the pattern for the cat's ear (picture 2).

picture 2

8. Pin the tracings to the red felt. Cut out the tracings and remove the pins.

9. Make one tracing of the pattern for the cat's tongue (picture 3).

10. Pin the tracing to the red felt. Cut out the tracing and remove the pins.

picture 3

11. BEFORE YOU START TO SEW: Arrange the ears, tongue, eyes (the blue buttons), and the nose (the red button) on the cat's face (see picture 4). Make a small chalk mark where each piece should be sewn.

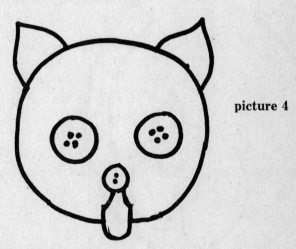

picture 4

12. Then sew on the blue buttons with blue thread, and the red button with red thread (see page 4).

13. Sew the ears and the tongue on with red thread. Use an overcast stitch (see page 5). (If you want to add whiskers on the cat's face, sew them in with white thread. Use a running stitch (page 5).

14. Pin the two pieces of black felt together with the cat's face on top.

15. Use black thread to sew the pieces together with a small running stitch (page 5). Double the thread and knot the end. Keep the stitches small and close to the outside edge. STOP sewing when you have two inches left to sew.

16. Remove the pins and fill the bag with beans. Then sew up the opening.

Christmas Ornaments

Giving Christmas ornaments is a
nice way to say "Merry Christmas"
year after year after year.

Christmas Star

You'll need

2 pieces of red felt 4 by 4 inches
white embroidery thread
embroidery needle
glue-on paper stars
polyester fiberfill for stuffing
pins
scissors
tracing paper and pencil

1. Trace the pattern for the star (picture 1).

2. Put the two pieces of red felt together. Pin the tracing to the double thickness of felt.

3. Cut out the tracing and remove the pins.

picture 1

4. Start sewing the two stars together with the white embroidery thread. Use an overcast stitch (see page 5). Make the stitches as small as you can. STOP sewing when there is only one side of a star point left to sew.

5. Take small amounts of stuffing and push them into the star. Use the pencil to get the stuffing down into all the points. Try to stuff the star evenly so there aren't any lumps.

6. Press the edges of the opening together and sew it closed.

7. Glue a paper star on the front and back.

8. To hang the star: Cut off a 6-inch piece of embroidery thread. Thread the needle but don't knot the thread. Push the needle through one of the points of the star. Slip the needle off the thread. Make the two ends of the thread even (picture 2). Tie a knot, then knot the ends of the threads together.

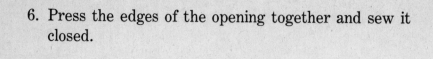

picture 2

Gingerbread Man

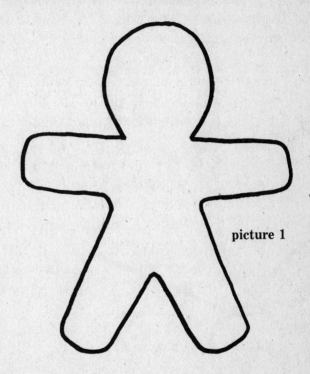

picture 1

You'll need

2 pieces of brown felt 4 by 4 inches
scraps of white felt
white embroidery thread
embroidery needle
scissors
polyester fiberfill for stuffing
pins
tracing paper and pencil

1. Trace the pattern for the gingerbread man (picture 1).

2. Put the two pieces of brown felt together. Pin the tracing to the double thickness of felt.

3. Cut out the tracing and remove the pins.

4. Start sewing the two pieces of brown felt together with the white embroidery thread. Use an overcast stitch (page 5). Begin sewing at the top of the head. STOP sewing when you finish the second arm.

5. Cut out 6 tiny white felt dots — about the size of the ones in picture 2. Glue down 2 dots for the eyes, 1 for the mouth, and 3 for buttons.

6. Push a small amount of stuffing into the legs, arms, and body. Try to stuff the body evenly so there aren't any lumps. Use the pointed end of the pencil to push the stuffing into the arms and legs.

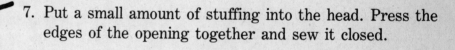

7. Put a small amount of stuffing into the head. Press the edges of the opening together and sew it closed.

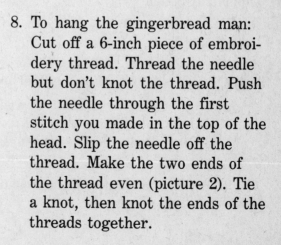

picture 2

8. To hang the gingerbread man: Cut off a 6-inch piece of embroidery thread. Thread the needle but don't knot the thread. Push the needle through the first stitch you made in the top of the head. Slip the needle off the thread. Make the two ends of the thread even (picture 2). Tie a knot, then knot the ends of the threads together.

Silvery Moon

picture 1

You'll need

a piece of blue felt 4 by 2 inches
a piece of white felt 4 by 2 inches
silver embroidery thread
embroidery needle
scissors
pins
polyester fiberfill for stuffing
tracing paper and pencil

1. Trace the pattern for the half moon (picture 1).

2. Pin the blue and white pieces of felt together. Pin the tracing to the double thickness of felt.

3. Cut out the tracing and remove the pins.

4. Start sewing the two moons together with the silver thread. Use an overcast stitch (see page 5). Make the stitches as small as you can. STOP sewing when there is about an inch left to sew.

5. Take small amounts of stuffing and push them into the moon. Use the pencil to get the stuffing down into the ends. Try to stuff the moon evenly so there aren't any lumps.

6. Press the edges of the opening together and sew it closed.

7. To hang the moon: Cut off a 6-inch piece of embroidery thread. Thread the needle but don't knot the thread. Push the needle through one end of the moon. Slip the needle off the thread. Make the two ends of the thread even (picture 2). Tie a knot, then knot the ends of the threads together.

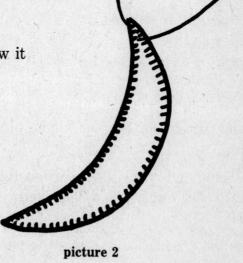

picture 2

48